ARIANNA'S MAGIC BOOTS VOL. 2

Underwater Sea Adventure

"Always Believe in yourself"

Karen Gasperini

By Karen A. Gasperini
Illustrations by Deanna McRae

Arianna's Magic Boots Vol. 2 Underwater Sea Adventure

by Karen A. Gasperini

Illustrations by Deanna McRae

©2017 Karen A. Gasperini

This book is dedicated to my daughter Arianna Ta'Mari Robinson and to the mermaids in my life my three nieces: Xzayah Mariana Garcia, Destiny Nereida Tantao, Carmela Annálize Gasperini, as well as my God-Daughter Lillian Sychel Young and all the other children of the world that like to pretend they're mermaid's or mermen, too.

Author's Thank you's

To my heavenly father for keeping me centered on this journey.

To my family and friends for their love & support.

Arianna jumps out of bed. She was super excited
to get ready for a beach day with her parents.
She gets dressed and hurries downstairs.

Next, she put on her leg braces which are
Ankle-foot orthosis (AFOs) and sneakers.
She calls them her "magic boots"
because they take her on adventures.

Arianna is excited for a day at the beach with her parents, she grabs her pail and shovel from the hall closet.

Off to the beach!

Arianna and her parents find the perfect spot to build a sand castle. "The mermaid castle is deep underwater," Arianna explains to her dad. "I wish I could go visit the mermaids." She closes her eyes, stomps three times and says, "Away we go."

When Arianna opens her eyes, she is deep under the
sea. Her magic boots turned into a mermaid tail.
She was a mermaid! Arianna squeals with delight!
She always wanted to be a mermaid.
She then sees three mermaids.

My name is Arianna. What's yours?" "We're sisters. The mermaid in blue says. My name is Xzayah, and this is Destiny, and our youngest sister is Carmela. "We're out looking for hidden underwater treasure to make into the perfect birthday gift for our big sister Lillian. She loves jewelry."

"Arianna, do you want to help us find the treasures
we need to finish for our sister's special gift?"
Carmela asks. "I would love to help." Arianna said.
She shows Arianna their list of items.

Arianna says to Destiny "That is a pretty seashell you're wearing on your ear." "It helps me hear sound underwater, it was made with mermaid magic along with Carmela's eye openers." Destiny says.

"Wow, we have something like that on land. We call them a hearing aid and glasses." Arianna explains.

First, they head to "Shell Cove" where they find lots of different seashells. Xzayah tells Carmela, "Count out five Ark seashells for Lillian's bracelet." Arianna offers to help. She's really good at counting.

Carmela and Arianna start counting out seashells.

Next, on the list, "Six white pearls." So the girls head to Pearl Mountain. It is the most beautiful sight Arianna has ever seen! The girls work together to find six white pearls.

☒ Five Ark seashells for Lillian's bracelet

☒ Six white pearls

☐ 1 glowing blue seahorse

There is only one goal left then they can work on putting Lillian's one of a kind bracelet together. The last item the girls need is from the secret underwater hot springs...a glowing blue seahorse.

The secret hot springs is warm and bright. The girls search the small ponds looking for the rare shell. They look everywhere.

"We're running out of time." "Lillian's birthday
party is going to start soon," said Carmela.
"Let's split up, so we can look faster," suggests
Destiny. Xzayah and Arianna swim to the right.
Destiny and Carmela swim to the left.

Arianna spots something bright in a little hole above a small crater in between some coral. It's the rare blue-glowing seahorse shell. Xzayah claps her hands with excitement. "Just in time for Lillian's party."

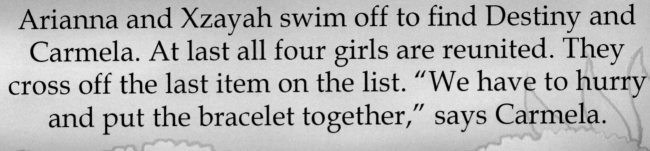

Arianna and Xzayah swim off to find Destiny and Carmela. At last all four girls are reunited. They cross off the last item on the list. "We have to hurry and put the bracelet together," says Carmela.

Destiny carefully strings the magical items together. Once all the pieces are in place the bracelet starts to glow a beautiful blue.

The girls do a celebration dance. Carmela sings,
"Join in, Arianna. We twirl, then clap, we twirl then
clap, we twirl then clap, and shout hooray!"

Xzayah stops. "We better go now before Lillian's birthday party starts." The girls race to make it in time for the party.

The friends
look for Lillian.

The three sisters yell, "Surprise!" and hand Lillian her present. Lillian is over the moon with joy. She hugs her little sisters. "Wow, this is a beautiful bracelet and my favorite color. I love it! Thank you," Lillian says.

Destiny says, "Guess what? We made a new friend.
This is Arianna." "She helped us make
your birthday surprise."

Lillian thanks Arianna with a hug.

"I better get going it's getting late," says Arianna. The sisters are sad but they understand Arianna can't stay. Carmela says, "We made this for you, Arianna. Thank you for all your help."

Arianna hugs her new friend's goodbye.

Then she closes her eyes and spins around three times before she says, "Away we go."

When Arianna opens her eyes she's back on the beach.
Her tail has turned back into her "Magic boots."

"Are you having fun?"
Arianna's mother asks.

Then Arianna jumps up and down. "Yes."
She puts the finishing touches on their castle.

Arianna and her parents celebrate with a dance.

"We twirl, then clap, we twirl then clap, we twirl then clap, and shout hooray!" Arianna says with a giggle.

"Where did you learn that from?" Arianna's dad asks. Arianna looks down at her new bracelet, smiles and says, "My new friends."

"Aww that's sweet. It's time to pack up and head home. We can come back another day." Says her mom. "Until our next adventure," Arianna says.

Author's Notes

"Arianna's Magic Boots," is based on Karen's daughter Arianna and herself. Growing up Karen and her daughter wore leg braces to help with their clubfeet. One of their favorite things to do when wearing their leg braces (AFOs) was using their imagination to go on adventures. Karen resides in Rhode Island with her family.

Arianna Age 5 with her little friend Pearl (2007)

Karen and her leg braces with her little brother Isaiah by her side. (1988)

38618612R00024

Made in the USA
Middletown, DE
10 March 2019